I0750868

BY-LAWS

OF THE

CHARLESTON

City Railway Company.

INCORPORATED, JAN. 28, 1861.

CHARLESTON, S. C.
Courier Job Press, 111 East Bay.
1866.

LIST OF OFFICERS.

President,

JOHN S. RIGGS.

Directors,

HENRY BUIST,	EDWARD WILLIS,
WM. L. TRENHOLM,	E. H. JACKSON,
HENRY T. PEAKE,	E. M. LAZARUS,

THOMAS J. WHARTON.

Superintendent,

E. H. JACKSON.

Secretary and Treasurer,

S. W. RAMSAY.

ACT OF INCORPORATION.

AN ACT

To incorporate the Charleston City Railway Company, of South Carolina.

I. *Be it enacted* by the Senate and House of Representatives, now met and sitting in General Assembly, and by the authority of the same, That Joshua Lazarus, John S. Riggs, David Riker, Thomas J. Wharton, and Henry Buist, and all those persons who may become members of the Charleston City Railway Company, of South Carolina, be, and the same are hereby declared a body politic and corporate, under the style and name of the Charleston City Railway Company, of South Carolina, and by that title shall have power to take, subscribe, and raise a capital stock to the amount of two hundred thousand dollars, in shares of fifty dollars each, if so much be necessary for the purposes contemplated, with power to increase the said capital to the further sum of three hundred thousand dollars, if found necessary: *Provided*, That such increase be assented to by a majority in number of the stockholders, who shall be notified, in two of the public papers of the city of Charleston, of a meeting to be held for that purpose.

II. That the said Charleston City Railway Company shall have power and authority, subject, as is hereinafter provided, to the ordinances, authority, and supervision of the City Council of Charleston relative thereto, to lay railway tracks through and along the streets within the corporate limits of the city of Charleston, and to use and employ upon such railway tracks sufficient and suitable carriages or cars, to be drawn by horses or animal power, for the transportation of passengers and freight, upon such rates as shall be fixed by the said company and approved of by the said City Council, and for this purpose shall have all the authority and power necessary to carry the same into effect.

III. That the said Charleston City Railway Company, of South Carolina shall be able and capable, by its corporate name, to buy property and to sell, for the purpose of its business, to sue and be sued, to plead and be impleaded, to answer and be answered unto, in any Court of Law or Equity in this State, to have succession of officers and members, and shall have power to make by-laws, not repugnant to the laws of the land, for the government and good order of its members, as shall be deemed expedient by a majority of the stockholders, and to have a common seal, and to alter and make new the same.

IV. That this Act shall remain in force and continue for the term of twenty-one years, and from thence until the expiration of the next session of the Legislature, and no longer.

V. That the said City Railway Company, before laying any railway tracks for the purpose of running cars thereon, in any street or streets in the city of Charleston, shall fully and formally submit their plan or plans, designating the street or streets on which they purpose to construct a railway, to the municipal authorities of said city, for their approval, and that all their works, along and through the streets of said city, be under the authority, supervision, and arrangement of the corporate authorities of the city of Charleston, subject to such provisions, contracts, ordinances, and restrictions as they may deem advisable for the general welfare and due protection of public and private rights, as also for the protection of the property and rights of said company.

VI. That the said City Railway Company shall have power and authority to issue bonds to an amount not exceeding fifty thousand dollars, the same to be redeemable at such time, not exceeding twenty years, as may be agreed upon by the said company, and to bear interest at the rate of seven per cent. per annum, payable semi-annually.

In the Senate House, the twenty-eighth day of January, in the year of our Lord one thousand eight hundred and sixty-one, and in the eighty-fifth year of the sovereignty and independence of the State of South Carolina.

WILLIAM D. PORTER, *President of the Senate.*
JAMES SIMONS, *Speaker House of Representatives.*

BY-LAWS

OF THE

CHARLESTON CITY RAILWAY COMPANY.

RULE I.

The office for the transaction of the business of the Company and general direction of its affairs shall be located in the City of Charleston.

RULE II.

The affairs of the Company shall be managed by a President and a Board of seven Directors. Four shall form a quorum

RULE III.

The annual meeting of the Stockholders, for the election of Directors, shall be held on the first Monday in November, in each year.

RULE IV.

The election for eight Directors shall be held on the first Monday in November, of each year, by two managers from among the Stockholders, who shall be appointed for that purpose, at any time previous to said election by the President. The polls shall be opened between the hours of ten and two o'clock, and each Shareholder shall be entitled to cast one vote for each share owned by him or her. The eight persons having the largest number of votes shall be, after the polls have been closed and the votes counted, declared duly elected.

The notice of the holding of the election shall be pnblished for at least one week before the day of election, in one or more of the news-papers in Charleston.

No person shall be elected a Director unless he shall be posessed in his own individual right of at least twenty-five shares. The President shall be elected at a meeting of the Directors to be held immediately after the result of the election shall have been announced

No Director shall be elected President unless he is the owner in his own right of fifty shares.

RULE V.

Special meetings of the Stockholders shall be called by the President through the Secretary and Treasurer, or at the request in writing to him of not less than two Stockholders, who shall in the aggregate, be the owners of seven hundred and fifty shares.

RULE VI.

Any vacancy or vacancies in the Board of Directors, by resignation or otherwise, may be filled for the unexpired term by the remaining Directors at any regular meeting of the Board.

RULE VII.

The President of the Company shall be elected by the Board of Directors from their own number; there shall also be elected by the Board a Secretary and Treasurer, and Superintendent. The Conductors, and such other officers as the business of the Company shall from time time to require, shall be appointed by the Superintendent, with the sanction of the President The Board of Directors shall fix the compensation of such officers as may be elected or appointed. In the absence of the President, the Board of Directors may appoint one of their number President *pro tempore*, who shall act in his lieu and stead.

RULE VIII.

It shall be the duty of the President to preside at all meetings of the Board of Directors, sign all Bonds, Certificates of Stock, contracts, and all other obligations entered into by the Company, and countersign all Checks for whatever moneys may be drawn from bank, or paid, and generally to perform all the acts incident to his office and enforce the By-Laws.

RULE IX.

It shall be the duty of the Secretary and Treasurer to prepare and keep proper books of accounts, stock books, and he shall countersign and register all Certificates of Stock and keep the corporate seal of the Company; shall sign receipts and acknowledgments for all moneys and other property of the Company which shall come into his hands, and disburse the same in accordance with the direction of the President; he shall give bonds with securities satisfactory to the Board of Directors for the faithful discharge of his duties, which Bond shall be held in the custody of the President of the Company;

he shall render, at each monthly meeting of the Board of Directors a balance-sheet of his accounts, and in case of his resignation or removal to deliver the Books and all other property of the Company over to his successor in office upon the written order of the President.

RULE X.

It shall be the duty of the Secretary to notify all meetings of the Stockholders and Directors, he shall record the proceedings of their respective meetings in proper books to be kept for that purpose, and he shall preserve the original minutes on file, and all other papers belonging to the Company.

RULE XI.

It shall be the duty of the Superintendent to take charge of all the real estate and personal property of the Company on the line of the Road, its branches, and connections ; to him will be entrusted the motive power and appurtenances employed thereon, the stables, depots, machinery, tools, material, and the cars ; and shall be held responsible for the same, and shall report from time to time as may be required by the President or Board, upon the condition of the Road, its equipment, and the property connected with the Road, and make such suggestions in relation to the same as the business of the Road or its importance to him may dictate.

RULE XII.

The Superintendent shall appoint, with the assent of the President, suitable persons as assistants in his department, and shall remove or suspend, at his discretion, or by direction of the President, reporting in such cases, the cause of such dismissal, if the same be required; and further make all necessary rules, and define the duties in detail of all subordinates; and all moneys received by him shall be paid over to the Secretary and Treasurer, with a statement of the same; andshall give good and sufficient security, to be approved of by the Board of Directors.

RULE XIII.

The seal of the Company shall be as as follows: the centre to have a cut representing a Street Car drawn by two Horses and the words "Charleston City Railway Company, Charleston, So. Ca.," encircling the outer edge.

RULE XIV.

All books, papers, correspondence, documents, and and files belonging to the Company in the hands of its officers shall be open to the inspection of the Directors.

RULE XV.

No Bond executed by any officer of the Company for the faithful discharge of his duties shall be signed as security by the President or any of the Directors.

RULE XVI.

The regular meetings of the Board of Directors shall be at the office of the Company at such hour as the President may deem best suited, on the first Monday of every month; special meetings of the Board shall be called by the Secretary and Treasurer whenever directed so to do by the President or any two members of the Board in writing, of which meeting the Secretary and Treasurer shall give at least one day's notice to the Directors by advertisement in the papers, or by written notice.

RULE XVII,

These By-Laws may be added to, altered, or amended at any regular or special meeting of the Stockholders, only by a vote of a majority of the whole Stock of the Company, thirty days notice of said change having been previously given.

www.ingramcontent.com/pod-product-compliance
Lightning Source LLC
LaVergne TN
LVHW020639110826
845149LV00004B/1279

* 9 7 8 1 4 1 8 1 9 0 3 7 8 *